HOLIDAY MEADOW

Books by
Edith M. Patch

NATURE STUDY

Dame Bug and Her Babies

Hexapod Stories

Bird Stories

First Lessons in Nature Study

Holiday Pond

Holiday Meadow

Holiday Hill

Holiday Shore

Mountain Neighbors

Desert Neighbors

Forest Neighbors

Prairie Neighbors

NATURE AND SCIENCE READERS

Hunting

Outdoor Visits

Surprises

Through Four Seasons

Science at Home

The Work of Scientists

HOLIDAY MEADOW

by

Edith M. Patch

YESTERDAY'S CLASSICS

ITHACA, NEW YORK

This edition, first published in 2020 by Yesterday's Classics, an imprint of Yesterday's Classics, LLC, is an unabridged republication of the text originally published by The Macmillan Company in 1935. For the complete listing of the books that are published by Yesterday's Classics, please visit www.yesterdaysclassics. com. Yesterday's Classics is the publishing arm of Gateway to the Classics which presents the complete text of hundreds of classic books for children at www.gatewaytotheclassics.com.

ISBN: 978-1-63334-048-0

Yesterday's Classics, LLC
PO Box 339
Ithaca, NY 14851

CONTENTS

I. Holiday Meadow. 1

II. "Spring Is Here". 4

III. Daucus 13

IV. Whistling Wejack. 26

V. A Bubble Blower. 41

VI. Hay Day 48

VII. Star Nose. 59

VIII. The Adventures of a Meadow
       Caterpillar 69

IX. Snowflakes. 83

X. The Silk Funnel 97

Sandy looked back with a question and invitation in his eyes.

CHAPTER I

HOLIDAY MEADOW

THERE is an open grassy field so crowded with flowers that the summer winds blowing over it are loaded with fragrance. A bobolink, gay in black and white and yellow, takes happy flights. He sings as he goes and his joyful music is like clear and sudden laughter. Then a meadowlark calls slowly a few sweet piping notes.

You do not need a map to tell you how to reach this place. It is along a pleasant country road that leads north or south or east or west. You can tell when you find it by the scent of the blossoms and by the songs of the birds and by the happy feeling you have when you look at it. Then you say, "Why, this must be Holiday Meadow!"—and sure enough it is!

Young dog, Sandy, knows one way to the meadow. He trots across a little brook on a rough bridge of old logs and planks. He looks back with a question and an invitation in his eyes. "Coming?" he seems to ask.

If you go with Sandy, he will be glad of your company for a while. Soon, however, he is likely to forget everything else in his hurry to find the nest of a mouse under a hummock of dry grass. Sandy would do well to be careful how he digs into that nest; for it may be that the mouse has moved out and that bumblebees have set up housekeeping there instead.

A crow flies scouting over the field. When he sees you he calls "Caw" several times in a way that seems to mean "Who comes here?"

Two little animals hear him and stand up on their hind legs while they look and listen and sniff. One is Wejack, the ground-hog, who presently slips into the doorway of his tunnel. The other is a rabbit with

The children named the cow "Daisy."

a quivery nose who decides to hide under the thorny tangle of blackberry branches by the pasture wall.

But Daisy, the young cow, does not heed the crow. She comes straight across the meadow to meet you. She likes boys and girls. When she was a little calf the children at Holiday Farm played with her and fed her. They named her "Daisy" for the white flowers with yellow centers that grow so thick in the field. Daisy, herself, does not care for these pretty blossoms. She much prefers the taste of grass.

Indeed Daisy takes little interest in many of the meadow affairs. She does not wonder how the frothy masses of bubbles come to be on the grass stems or what may be inside of them. She does not guess what the Black Swallowtail butterfly puts on the under side of a caraway leaf. She never watches a slender green grasshopper to see how he makes music with the edges of his wings. She does not find out what happens when . . .

*   *   *   *   *

The field across which Daisy comes to meet you is full of puzzles. The more answers you can find by hunting and watching the better you will enjoy your holiday in a meadow.

CHAPTER II

"SPRING IS HERE"

MAGNA, the meadowlark, was sitting on the broken top of an old tree trunk which stood at the edge of Holiday Meadow. The upper parts of his feather coat were mostly dark. His throat and breast were bright yellow. Between the yellow of his throat and the yellow of his breast he wore a black bib shaped somewhat like a new moon.

"Spring is here!" Magna's voice was sweet and a bit sad-sounding. The singer, himself, was not sorry about anything, though. He was happy. He was glad to be home again at Holiday Meadow. Perhaps he had spent his winter in Maryland or perhaps not so far south. He did not mind rather cold weather.

It was pleasant for Magna that he did not feel chilly while he sat on top of the old tree trunk that first day of April. For it was a nipping sort of morning. The air was cold. When Magna opened his mouth and sang, his breath came out in white frosty puffs. It showed plainly because the sky beyond was clear deep blue.

If you had been there at six o'clock that morning you could have seen the bird's song while you were hearing it. That is it would have seemed like seeing a

"Spring is here," sang Magna, the meadowlark.

song,—with the notes floating up from the bird's mouth like frosted music.

"Spring is here!" Magna sang his song again and again. Way up the road a bird like him was sitting on the tip of a telegraph pole. He was singing rather slowly. He sounded as if he was saying, "Swe-e-et spri-i-ng is he-ere!"

Over by the pasture a third bird was perched on top of a fence post. He was calling in a quick voice, "Spring's here!"

Young Dick, in his room at Holiday Farm, rubbed his eyes and then sat up in bed to listen. A few minutes later he was rapping on his cousin's door.

"Wake up, you lazy Anne," he called, "and look and listen out of the hall window."

Anne pulled on her warm bath robe and joined her cousin at the open window. First she looked, and what she saw was a fresh sprinkling of snow that had fallen on Holiday Meadow the evening before. Next she listened, and what she heard was "Spring is here!" "Swe-e-et spri-i-ng is he-ere!" "Spring's here!"

Then Anne danced on her toes and said, "The meadowlarks have come—three of them and each with his own way of telling us that spring is here." And Anne was so glad that her voice sounded like a song, too.

Dick chuckled. "Doesn't look much like spring with last night's snow, does it? And see our breath going out of the window, all white and frosty!"

"Spring is here!" sang Magna.

The cousins laughed. "I think that is his April Fool Song, to-day," said Anne.

Dick and Anne had learned from their bird book that the meadowlarks of western prairies had much longer and sweeter songs than those that came to Holiday Meadow. The cousins hoped that some time they might visit places where they could hear the full rich music of the western meadowlarks. Meanwhile they enjoyed Magna's song—what there was of it.

It was a short tune, to be sure, but he sang it a great

6

many times. One of his favorite singing places was the top of the old broken tree where he perched the first day of April, but often he sang while he was standing on the ground. Sometimes he sang a warbly sort of twitter while he was flying.

Early in the season Magna met his mate and they passed pleasant days together. For a while they were most interested in their nest.

They did not make a hanging nest like the one a pair of orioles put on a swinging branch of an elm that stood in the yard of Holiday Farm. They did not attach their nest to a low willow bush over in Holiday Swamp as did a pair of red-winged blackbirds. They built their nest on the ground.

Even though it was in a different sort of place, the nest of Magna and his mate was, in one respect, somewhat like the nest in the elm and the one in the swamp bush. All three nests were carefully woven. Perhaps it is because meadowlarks and orioles and blackbirds are rather closely related that they all weave their nests, instead of making them with sticks laid criss-cross as some other birds do.

Magna's mate found a house lot that suited her exactly. There was a little hollow just right to fit a nest into. Close to the hollow grew a tall tuft of sheltering grass. This house lot was near one edge of the meadow not too far from the swamp where a thirsty bird could find a shallow stream and drinking pools. A water supply is as important to a bird as it is to a person.

When the nest was finished it had coarse grass on

the outside and fine grass on the inside, and it had a dome-shaped roof of woven grass. Of course all the grass in the nest was brown and dry. That is, it was dry when the nest was finished. But while Mrs. Magna was working on it she used damp grass fibers which were so soft they could be woven without breaking. She gathered these in the morning while they were wet with dew. Afterward the grass dried in the sunshine.

It was a charming nest.

8

It was a charming nest even while it was empty. But about a week later when it had six eggs in it, it was such a dear nest that Mother Magna could not bear to leave it except when she was very thirsty or very hungry indeed. The rest of the time she brooded her eggs and kept them warm. They were white eggs with brown and purple speckles on them.

Dick and Anne had been watching the meadow through their bird glasses and had noticed that Magna quite often alighted near a certain spot when he flew down to the meadow. They thought that he was visiting Mother Magna.

One day Dick said, "Let's go and find the meadow-lark's nest." When they reached the place near where Magna had disappeared, the bird flew up from the ground. While he was flying he showed the white outer feathers of his short tail. He went to the broken tree and called "Yert" in an anxious voice. That was his way of warning Mother Magna of danger.

The cousins walked slowly and were careful where they stepped. They hunted for more than an hour without finding the nest. Then Anne said, "Let's stop. That poor old meadowlark is staying on guard in the tree and he is worried. I'm worried, too. There is so much dry grass next the ground that it would be easy to step on a hidden nest without seeing it. If we do, we'll be sorry all summer."

"All right," said Dick, "we can go to the swamp and hunt for the red-winged blackbird's nest. There is no danger of stepping on that. Maybe there will be eggs to see now, and later we can visit the young birds and see how fast they grow."

Magna watched Dick and Anne walk toward the swamp. When they had gone far enough so that he no longer felt anxious about his mate and her nest, he stopped calling "Yert" and flew down to the meadow to hunt for food.

The old bird had a keen appetite and enjoyed stalking along in the tall grass to find something to eat. But it was not until the speckled eggs had hatched that his hunting season began in earnest. Then Father Magna hunted from dawn until dusk.

For there were six mouths always open to give him a hungry greeting when he went to the nest. And much fresh meat must be poked into those mouths before the young birds could grow up and be able to do their own hunting.

The food that was best for the young meadowlarks was insect-meat. Magna caught grasshoppers, both old ones with wings and young ones without. He pounced on grown moths and young caterpillars. He picked up beetles and grubs.

And every time he carried insects to the nest, he found six little birds with mouths wide open and ready to swallow what he brought.

Of course Magna did not provide all the family meals. Mother Magna was as good a hunter as he was and she kept as busy. As soon as her eggs were hatched she did not need to stay on the nest. So she hurried here and there and did her full share of the day's hunting.

When the Man of Holiday Farm saw these birds busy in the meadow he smiled. "The meadowlarks help take care of the hay," he said. "Most of the insects they catch are such as feed on grass. So the more of these birds there are in the field, the better the hay crop will be."

Daisies are pretty but they do not make good hay.

Each time Magna and Mother Magna went to feed their young ones they brushed against the woven roof of the nest from the outside. Each time the growing birds reached up for food they brushed against the roof from the inside. The dome-shaped top was not very strong, so before the birds were ready to leave the nest they were without any roof to cover them. However, they did not really need a roof, so they were well enough off without it.

Besides they were growing rapidly for their diet of insects agreed with them. In due time they were too big and strong to stay crowded together in so small a home.

One day when Dick and Anne were running along the edge of the meadow, eight birds flew up ahead of them. They all showed white outer tail feathers. One of the birds went to the top of the old broken tree and said "Yert" in an anxious voice. One of them alighted on a fence post and moved her tail in a fidgety way. The other six flew a little way over the grass and then dropped to the ground as if they were a bit tired.

"Look," said Dick, "those must be the young meadowlarks. Perhaps that is the first time they ever flew. They did not go far. Aren't you glad they are out of the nest before it is time to cut the hay?"

Just then Magna sang from the top of his tree. "Spring is here!" was what his song sounded like to the cousins.

"It is summer, now, old chap," Anne called to him, "and next it will be fall."

"Perhaps," said Dick thoughtfully, "it always seems like spring to a meadowlark—when he is happy."

CHAPTER III

DAUCUS

In her early life Daucus was a seed. At that time she had a stiff coat with rows of barbed prickles on it. She wore this strange spiny baby coat for more than half a year.

At first she lived with seven or eight hundred sister seeds in a hollow cup-shaped cluster that looked somewhat like a bird's nest. This seed-cluster grew at the tip of a wild carrot stem. There were many of these plants, each with several such stems, in a weedy field not far from Holiday Farm.

During the frosty fall weather the stems and the "birds' nests" at their tips became dry and brown. Later, when the winter storms came, the snow often piled in little fluffy white mounds on top of the nests. Sometimes the snow would be blown off by the wind while it was light. At other times it would melt a bit during the sunny part of the day and then freeze at night in icy crusts. Then when morning came the seed-clusters looked as if they were in sparkling glass cases.

Little Daucus never knew whether the winter days were sunny or stormy. She and the hundreds of sister seeds slept in the brown nest on the tip of the slender stem. They stayed there until nearly March. Then one

Blossoms and "Birds' Nests"

day a blustering wind snapped the brittle stem and broke off the nest of seeds.

Away the round cluster rolled over the crusty snow like a feather ball before the wind! And all about were other similar clusters scurrying in the same direction.

Dick and Anne were coming home from school that afternoon while the field looked as if the winds there were playing a game with the little round balls.

"See," said Anne, "the birds' nests have broken off the wild carrot plants and they are rolling along like tumble-weeds."

14

"They are blowing toward Holiday Meadow. Let's race with them!" said Dick.

Just as Dick spoke, the seed-cluster with Daucus in it blew by and the cousins began to run. Daucus reached Holiday Meadow first. But the slope near the river was sheltered a bit from the wind; and the children overtook Daucus there.

The slope near the river was covered with Queen Anne's lace.

"I'll beat you to the bottom of the slope," Anne said to the seed-ball with a laugh. But just then she slipped on an icy spot and sat down on top of Daucus's ball.

When Anne stood up she saw that the frail cluster

was crushed and mixed with broken snow crust. So the cousins chose another ball with which to race.

Daucus was not harmed by the accident. Her hard coat protected her. But a lump of icy snow had rolled on top of her and held her still. The wind could not blow her any farther. She had reached the end of her journey.

In due time spring days came. Melted snow soaked the ground of Holiday Meadow and fresh rain fell. Daucus's coat was wet. Her little seed-body was moistened by water and warmed by sunshine; and it began to grow. She pushed sprouting roots down into the ground. She reached tiny leaves up into the air. She no longer needed her baby clothes.

The meadow slope was well drained and the ground did not stay too wet for the best health of wild carrot plants. So, before her first summer was over, Daucus had a tough pale yellow tap-root shaped somewhat like a scrawny little carrot; and she had a crown of beautiful feathery leaves. She did not have any tall stems and flowers; for, unlike many kinds of plants, wild carrots wait until their second summer before they blossom.

Although Daucus had no flowers that summer, she did have a butterfly for a guest. Of course the butterfly did not visit the green leaves for nectar. She came on a different sort of errand. One day at noon when the sun was bright she stopped for about a quarter of a minute on one of Daucus's soft feathery leaves. During that brief call she glued one egg to the under side of the leaf.

She was a rather large butterfly. When she spread her wings they measured more than three inches from the tip of the right fore wing to the tip of the left one. She was a beautiful creature whose black velvety wings were bordered by two rows of yellow spots. On the hind wings there were spots of pale blue on the black space between the yellow rows. Each hind wing was tipped with a slender black tail.

After Black Swallowtail, for that was her name, left Daucus she flew to a caraway leaf and glued one egg to the under side of that.

The carrot and the caraway both belong to the Parsley Family; and it is a wonderful fact that Black Swallowtail butterflies never lay an egg on any plant that does not belong to that family. They may leave their eggs, one in a place, on parsnip or dill or celery or parsley or other plants of this family; but they never waste their eggs by putting them on other kinds of leaves.

Of course you would like to know how a Black Swallowtail chooses plants of one family from all the other plants of fields and gardens. So should I. But no one can tell us exactly for no one has the senses of a butterfly. People think that when she is ready to lay her eggs, carrots and related plants have for her such an attractive scent that she cannot help stopping at such leaves.

All the plants belonging to the Parsley Family have certain likenesses in the shapes of their flowers. Perhaps to a Black Swallowtail they have the same sort of odor. Even to a human nose certain of these plants have somewhat similar smells.

If you wish to find out what plants belong to the

Parsley Family you might follow a Black Swallowtail. That would be one way to study botany.

It is fortunate for the caterpillar youngsters of Black Swallowtail butterflies that their mothers never mislay their eggs, for leaves of plants belonging to the Parsley Family are the only sorts of food that agree with them.

A handsome caterpillar who likes celery and other plants of the Parsley Family.

When a tiny caterpillar crept out of the eggshell that had been left on Daucus's leaf he made himself quite at home; and as soon as he felt hungry, he helped himself to carrot-leaf salad.

He did not waste any of his food but ate every bit that he cut off with his little tooth-like jaws. So he grew rather fast.

At first he was black with some white marks and rows of little fleshy spines; but by the time he was in his last caterpillar stage he was much more handsome. His skin was then smooth and gayly colored. He was green with cross-bands of black and on each black band was a row of orange spots. He had two soft orange-colored horns but these were usually drawn in under the skin just behind his head and did not show.

One day a young bird, not yet much used to hunting for itself, saw this bright-colored caterpillar and poked him with its beak. When the bird touched him he thrust out his horns quickly and the air all about him was filled with a strange strong odor. The young bird did not like that smell and went away in a hurry. Left to himself, the caterpillar drew in his horns and crept along the leaf.

Daucus's nearest plant neighbor was an older wild carrot, one of whose lower blossom stems was resting across the feathery leaf on which the caterpillar was creeping. When he touched this stem he climbed up on it and began to munch the leaves he found there.

It was fortunate for Daucus that the caterpillar went when he did for he had grown old enough to need larger and larger carrot-leaf salads to satisfy his greedy appetite. The hungry visitor, however, had left Daucus enough of her feathery leaves so that her health was

*One day Daucus's guest stopped being a caterpillar
and became a chrysalis.*

not injured. Her hardy tap-root was well and strong when fall came.

She rested quietly all winter and when the snow had melted and the ground was warmed by the spring sunshine she began her second season's growth.

Instead of having just a single tuft of leaves, as she had when she was one summer old, she grew a long branching leafy stem. At the tip of this stem and at the end of each branch there was a large compound cluster of small flowers. The slender little flower-stalks which formed a cluster started from a common center like the ribs of an open umbrella.

Such a blossom cluster is called an umbel. Since members of the Parsley Family have their flowers growing in this manner they are called umbel-bearing plants.

Wild carrot blossoms are white or very pale creamy yellow or sometimes tinged with light pink. And in the center of each large flat umbel is one flower (and sometimes several) of a dark rich red color.

All of Daucus's blossom clusters were like that except one of them. The flat cluster of blossoms that grew at the tip of her main stem was different from all the rest of her clusters. It was, indeed, different from all the other wild carrot clusters in Holiday Meadow. This cluster had a whole three-cornered section of dark red flowers which reached from the center of the umbel to the outer edge.

This flower-cluster of Daucus's was so different from ordinary wild carrot blossoms that you may call it a "freak" or an "oddity" if you like. Perhaps no other wild carrot in the world ever had one exactly like it.

People have long admired the fine lacy blossoms of wild carrot. One name given the plant many years ago and still used is "Queen Anne's Lace." The graceful leaves have had their share of admiration, too. It is said that in the time of James I the court ladies wore them for plumes.

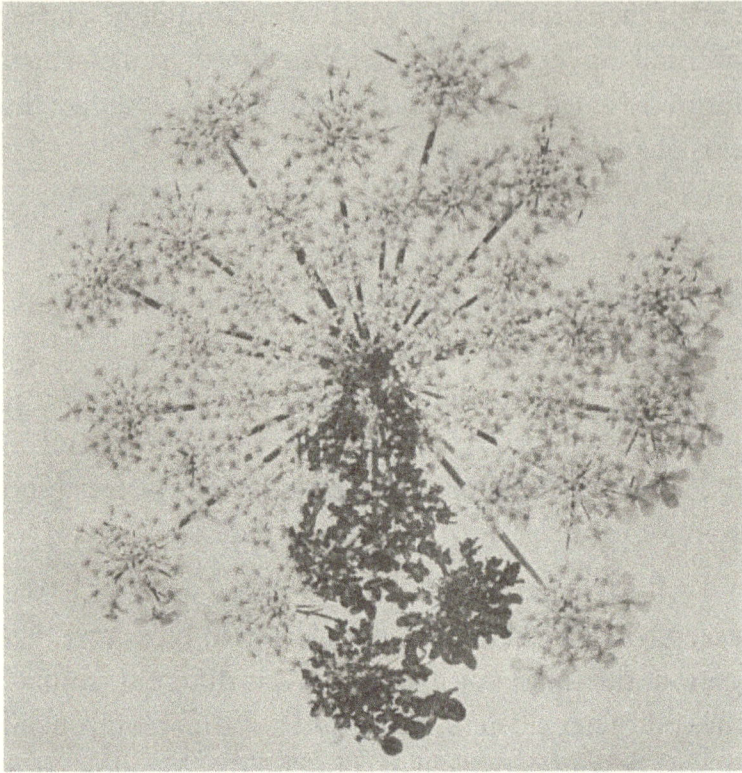

This blossom had a whole section of dark flowers.

One day when Dick and his cousin were walking through Holiday Meadow they decided to find out how wild carrots tasted. So they dug up some of the tap-roots and were carrying them to the house when they met Uncle David.

"They are rather scraggly and lean looking," said Anne, "but I think I'll cook them so we can eat some for dinner."

"Please don't," said Uncle David, "that would be an unwise experiment."

"Why?" asked Dick.

"Well, it is commonly thought that wild carrots are poisonous."

"Are they really?" asked Anne.

"I do not know," replied her uncle. "I have often wondered whether some one once tasted a raw tough second-season root and it did not agree with him or whether even the cooked young roots are somewhat poisonous. But I never wanted so much to know that I was willing to find out by eating them, myself."

"You see," he went on, "the Parsley Family includes many plants that are not fit for food for man or beast and some of them are deadly dangerous.

"Poison hemlock is one of these. If cows eat the tender young leaves in the spring, they die. Children have died from eating the seeds which they mistook for those of the caraway. The 'cup of death' which was given to Socrates in Athens many centuries ago is thought to have been a brew of poison hemlock.

"Water hemlock is quite as bad. Its fleshy roots are said to have rather a pleasant taste, but one root is enough to kill a cow, and a person would risk death by eating a very little piece of a root."

Uncle David looked down at the roots Dick still held in his hand. Then he said gravely, "Some of the poisonous relatives of the parsley are not easily told from the harmless ones. Suppose we have an agreement that you two youngsters refrain from eating seeds, leaves or roots of wild umbel-bearers until you know more about them than you do at present."

"All right," said Dick, "only I don't understand about carrots. I thought I was being careful. I read my plant book and it said that garden carrots were descended from wild carrots."

"Most botanists believe that that is so," said his uncle, "and they call both the wild Queen Anne's lace and the cultivated carrot by the same name *(Daucus Carota).*

"It may be that in a certain locality in Europe some of the wild plants had plumper, more tender and better tasting roots than other strains. It may be some such variety that was first cultivated and continued to have edible roots. It is not unlikely that the *roots* of these wild plants differ somewhat in appearance and quality. You see how different this *blossom* is from all the others in the field." And he pointed to Daucus's freak flower-cluster.

First the seed-cluster is flat, then like a bird's nest, then like a ball.

Perhaps (who knows?) if the seeds of Daucus's rich red blossoms had ripened and grown, her daughter plants might have had dark flower-clusters and Holiday Meadow might have had a new color of Queen Anne's lace!

One day as the clusters of green unripe seeds were becoming hollow like cups or birds' nests Dick and Anne heard their uncle say to his helper, "That meadow slope isn't fit for hay. Better plow the weeds under before the seeds are ripe. We'll put cultivated crops into that piece of land for a few years before we seed it to grass again."

Then the cousins remembered the gusty winter day when they had raced with the tumbling "birds' nests."

"They have been *jolly* weeds!" said Dick with a grin.

CHAPTER IV

WHISTLING WEJACK

ONE of his names was Wejack. One was Woodchuck. One was Ground-hog. One was Marmot. He had other names, too; though four seem enough, especially as he, himself, did not know any of the names people gave him. When he talked he did not speak in words. He spoke in whistles. That is why Anne and Dick called him "Whistling Wejack." He lived in Holiday Meadow.

Holiday Meadow is a long field that reaches from the margin of Holiday Stream to the foot of Holiday Hill.

Whistling Wejack lived at the end of the meadow nearest the hill. His home was a long underground tunnel and it had two doorways. One of these opened into a garden full of clover in the meadow. The other was hidden by rocks.

Dick and Anne and little dog Sandy knew where Wejack's garden hole was; but the hole between the rocks was so placed that no person or dog could get to it.

Sandy's chief interest in Wejack was the fun of sniffing down the opening of the tunnel and trying excitedly to dig the woodchuck out. Wejack did not

Whistling Wejack

seem much worried by the dog's activities. His tunnel was long and his private doorway among the rocks at the other end was as well guarded as a strong castle. In fact Wejack sometimes lay quietly on top of the rocks, sunning himself, while he watched Sandy pawing frantically at the hole far away in the clover garden.

Dick and Anne, however, did not care to disturb Wejack's home. They wished to become acquainted with him. So, usually, when they went to call on the woodchuck, they put Sandy in the shed and shut the door.

One day the cousins saw Wejack on top of his favorite rock at the foot of the hill. When they came rather near he slipped out of sight so quickly that they were not sure which way he went.

Now that they knew where he liked to sun himself they often came to visit him. Wejack would see them coming and would lie motionless. Unless they came too near he did not go away to hide. He hid in plain sight—just by keeping still. At such times he seemed like a part of the brown and gray shadows on the rock, and sometimes Dick and Anne used to look right at him without seeing him at all.

He seemed like a part of the rock.

When they told Uncle David how hard it was to see the woodchuck, he explained that many wild creatures have a way of hiding by keeping motionless. "That method of escaping notice is called 'freezing,'" he said, "because the animal stays as still as if it were frozen and could not move."

Wejack played the "Freezing Game."

So Dick and Anne learned to "freeze" by watching how the woodchuck did the trick; and they found that birds and squirrels and rabbits and porcupines and other little wild creatures came quite near them when they stayed "frozen" long enough. In that way they saw a great deal more of the animals than they could if they had been walking up the hill and talking.

The easiest way for them to play their "Freezing

Game" was to sit down comfortably on the ground with their backs against a rock or a big tree trunk. Then, as long as they kept their hands and feet and heads still and did not fidget or whisper, they were all right. At such times the woodchuck used to come and go among the rocks or run down to feed in the clover as if there were no one near him.

But as soon as they became tired of keeping so quiet and wriggled a little, then Wejack would look at them at once. Next he would stand still and whistle at them. Perhaps he was trying to scare them away but they were never frightened by his music. His whistling sound was clear and rather sweet and they liked it.

The woodchuck had another habit the children liked. When he stood on his hind legs he always dropped his front paws. Dick and Anne giggled the first time they saw him do this. "He looks too silly for words!" said Dick. "Just like a person who is trying hard to be graceful with his hands," remarked Anne, as she mimicked him.

Of course Wejack was not really trying to be graceful. His little paws dropped naturally in a pretty way.

After the grass grew tall in the meadow, Dick and Anne used sometimes to hide where they could see Wejack's front doorway in the clover garden. Beside this was a large mound of dirt that Wejack had piled there when he was digging his tunnel.

Sometimes they crept through the grass so slowly and quietly that Wejack did not know they were there.

At least sometimes he did not know until the crow told him.

Of course Corbie, the crow, did not say, "Look out, Wejack, two children are creeping through the grass toward your hole." All Corbie did was to call, "Caw! Caw! Caw!" and the chances are that he was not thinking about Wejack at all.

As a matter of fact it was Corbie's job to watch the meadow and warn the other crows when people went abroad. So when he saw the cousins from Holiday Farm he said, "Caw!" three times and flew to a tall pine on the hill while he looked to see where they were going.

A crow's signal may be intended only for the other crows. But almost all the wild creatures of meadow and hillside and woodland recognize the warning. When a crow caws three times in a certain tone he means what a person would mean if he yelled, "Danger! Look out!"

Wejack, of course, could not see very far through the tall meadow grass. At such times he depended a great deal on Corbie's signals. Whenever he heard the warning voice of the sentinel crow he would stand erect on his hind legs in sudden alarm, gazing and sniffing first this way and then that, as if sure that danger must be near.

It was while Dick and Anne were sitting, one day, close enough to the mound to see Wejack as he stood so before his open doorway, that they saw, too, the woodchuck's wonderful vanishing trick. The children

Wejack sniffed the air for danger.

were keeping as quiet as they could, but it was rather hard for them to stay "frozen" long where they had nothing to lean against; and after a while they moved a little,—enough so that Wejack glanced at them. They breathed only short breaths and were so quiet that the woodchuck did not seem frightened. He did not dash quickly into his hole headfirst as he would have done if he were being chased.

Indeed, he did not seem to be moving at all. He sank backward bit by bit so slowly that even while they watched, Dick and Anne could hardly see a motion; only where there had been a woodchuck, erect with drooping paws, there was at last only a hole in the ground.

The children crept, very carefully, to the mound. For a moment near the top of the black hole they saw Wejack's bright eyes gleaming at them. Then even the eyes were gone!

One spring morning Uncle David came into the house and remarked, "A troublesome ground-hog has been visiting our vegetable garden and eating most of the early planting of peas."

"That must be our Polly Woodchuck," began Anne calmly. "She likes vegetables—*especially* peas. I saw her this morning when I went out to see the sun come up. Polly was eating her breakfast of young pea vines." Then Anne's voice trembled a little. "I thought I'd tell you," she said, "that Polly can have my share and I'll go without green peas this summer."

Dick looked at his uncle's face. There was almost a frown in his forehead and almost a smile at the corners of his mouth. "We'll chase Polly over to the hill, Uncle David, where she will not damage the garden any more!" he said quickly.

Polly had three holes opening from her tunnel. One was quite near the end of the peas in the garden. Two were under stone piles in the hedgerow between the garden and the meadow. The children had been watching the woodchuck for several days and knew where she ran when Sandy chased her.

It took the cousins all the morning to move the

stones away from Polly's holes in the hedgerow. They carried a lot of the small stones to the garden and rolled them into the opening that was near the peas. Then they plugged the end of one of the other holes. The third one they left open so that Polly could come out easily without digging a new hole.

Polly stayed in her tunnel nearly all day. The noises near her doorways had frightened her. But late in the afternoon as all seemed quiet, she came out of her one free hole and stood up and looked out. She rested one paw against the trunk of a tree and let the other droop. She turned her head and listened with her short ears. After a while she gave a long churr-rr-rr-ing whistle.

Dick, who was sitting on a branch of a big apple-tree near the hedgerow, heard her. He thought it was a lonesome sounding whistle. Then from far up the meadow he heard another woodchuck calling. Polly heard the sound, too, and trotted along the meadow toward the hill.

Dick climbed down the tree and packed little stones into the remaining doorway of Polly's dugout. "Of course she can dig other holes if she wishes to do it," he thought, "but maybe she will not care to come back. She hasn't had a very pleasant day here."

That evening at supper time, Uncle David asked, "What's the latest news of Polly?"

"Oh," said Dick cheerfully, "Whistling Wejack met her in the meadow and I think he invited her over to the hill."

The Rocks of Holiday Hill

Dick's guess was right. Polly did not come back to the garden. Instead she helped Wejack improve his home. They dug several more branches to his tunnel so as to have more doorways when they wished to go in or out. They made three or four little dugout chambers or dens in widened places in the tunnel. In these they spread comfortable beds of dry stubble and leaves. They found their bedding in the meadow and on the hill and they carried it home in their mouths. Sometimes they rested in one chamber and sometimes in another. They kept them all fresh and clean.

It was on a pleasant day in early summer, while Anne was sitting at the foot of the hill not far from one of Wejack's holes, that she saw seven little animals come out to play among the rocks.

They had fluffy bodies and very short legs. Their ears were little and their mouths drooped at the corners. They resembled Polly and Wejack but they were prettier and very small. They were lively little woodchucks and tumbled and rolled about on the ground, biting and hugging and tussling with one another in joyful frolic.

During their play they ran quite near to Anne. She kept very still. One of her hands was resting on the ground and in it was a half-eaten chocolate candy. Two

One of Polly and Wejack's Children

of the young woodchucks stopped near her and sniffed. Next they crept to her hand and tasted the candy. Then, quick as a flash, one of them pulled it out of her hand and went off with it.

Anne chuckled. "You darlings!" she said.

Wejack, all this time, had been sunning himself on his favorite rock. When Anne spoke, he looked at her and whistled softly. He did not seem very much worried. After all these weeks of seeing Anne frequently he was rather used to her. Besides, it did not seem to be his task to take care of his seven sons and daughters. Polly liked to do that.

Polly took care of them now. She stood up near a rock, resting her paws on top of it. When she saw Anne, she whistled a long shrill command. Her seven children understood what she said to them and ran pell-mell for their nearest hole.

After that Dick and Anne came nearly every pleasant day to see the young woodchucks. They brought crackers soaked in milk, and cookies and chocolate candy. After placing these dainties near Wejack's door they sat down not far away and "froze" while they waited for the little woodchucks to come out for their treat. At first the youngsters did not seem at all timid. They had not learned to be afraid of people. But Polly attended to their education and the more she whistled to them when Dick and Anne were near the more shy they became.

Mr. and Mrs. Wejack and the seven young Wejacks were very busy during the late summer and fall. They were getting food enough to last them all winter. They did not gather extra food and store it away as squirrels and muskrats and beavers and certain other of their relatives do. They prepared for winter as bears and raccoons do,—by eating as much as they could of the

Wejack sometimes found his way to the cornfield.

best tasting food they found and becoming very very fat indeed.

This marmot is a western relative of the eastern woodchuck.

Early in the season the woodchucks had enjoyed eating dandelion blossoms, but of course they did not find many of these flowers in the fall. There were plenty of other kinds, however. The late blossoms of red clover tasted good to them and they liked these even after the flowers went to seed. Indeed they ate the seeds of various plants including some grain. Seeds are fattening, you know, so the diet they chose naturally was the best sort for them.

By the time really cold weather came, the nine woodchucks were all so fat that their plump bodies were rather heavy for such short legs to carry. They seemed lazy in their motions. There came an extra chilly day, indeed, when they were too lazy to make any motions at all. They just lay curled up in the warm beds in their dens with their noses tucked under their round stomachs and slept.

Exactly how long they stayed there, I cannot tell you. There is a legend, as perhaps you know, that woodchucks always waken the second day of February and come out to test the weather. If the sun is shining, as it does on a snappy clear cold day, so the legend goes, the woodchucks see their shadows and return to their dens for another nap of six weeks.

Legends are most interesting though they cannot be taken for fact. This much, however, is certain,— these animals have that one day in the year named for them and February 2nd is known in our calendar as Ground-hog Day.

CHAPTER V

A BUBBLE BLOWER

OF COURSE you have blown a bubble, yourself, and watched the rainbow colors glimmer until the hollow beauty burst. But you never blew an air castle of bubbles and lived in it. Phil did, though, really and truly; and that is why his story is worth telling.

At first Phil was inside an egg his mother left all winter in Holiday Meadow. Although the thermometer went down to zero and the wind blew from the north, the egg was not injured in the least. It hatched just as well the next May, after being brooded by the winter snow and the spring sunshine, as the eggs of a fussy old biddy do, after being snuggled by a warm feathered breast for three weeks.

That seems a strange beginning; and the rest of Phil's life was no less wonderful. So we need not be surprised to find him, early in June, already dwelling in his air castle.

He was an orphan, living alone in his bubble house. He had brothers and sisters, plenty of them, and all were the same age as himself. But they did not live together. Each one lived alone in a bubble house within a stone's

Phil lived in an air castle like one of these.

throw of Phil. Not that he ever did throw a stone at any of them! He did not even look at them. As a matter of fact he did not know that he had brothers and sisters. He did no real thinking of any sort.

Not that Phil was brainless, you know; for he had a brain and nerves quite as useful for his needs as yours are for human purposes. He had a heart, too, a queer one shaped like a tube and lying along the middle of his back. When his blood flowed out of his heart it went loose almost anywhere in his body, like a stream in an open channel and not in veins and arteries like yours. His breathing was different, too. When he breathed he did not get his air through two holes in his head; but through a number of openings along the sides of his body. His muscles were rather strong, and the very strange thing about them was that they were fastened to a skeleton on the outside of his body instead of inside.

It was this skeleton of Phil's that gave him his only really troublesome moments; for the inside of his body grew faster than the outside could stretch. So he became squeezed somewhat as a person does whose clothes are too tight. If a person in that plight is sensible, he gets out of that snug suit and uses a bigger one. That is what Phil did with his skeleton when it pinched him too much.

It is not the easiest thing in the world to wriggle out of a skeleton; but all insects that grow up must molt several times in their lives, and so, of course, Phil managed to do it. He pushed with his body and the skeleton tore at the back. Then he pulled his head out of his skull and his six legs out of their boots. After that he crept out of his shell and stretched. When he had rested for a while he felt hungry and hardly stopped eating until his new skeleton had, in its turn, become too tight. Then he molted again.

Except at molting time Phil had nothing to trouble him and he spent the hours sipping his food and blowing his house.

Phil never chewed his food. He sucked it, somewhat as you drink lemonade through a straw. His mouth was a long hollow tube. It was jointed so that he could fold it against the under side of his body when he was not using it.

This little insect did not step outside of his bubble house at mealtime. When he was thirsty, which was nearly every minute, he thrust the sharp tip of his long mouth into the grass stem in the midst of his castle.

When you are walking out of doors, do you sometimes pull a stem of grass and nibble the sweet tender part at the tip? The sap that gives the grass stem a pleasant taste is the kind of juice Phil drank day after day while he was growing.

That juice is a wonderful liquid. It is the sap of life that flows in a grass stem and nourishes the growing plant from the time it is a tiny seedling until it is old enough to blossom and have seeds of its own. That seems enough for one kind of juice to do but it can do even more. When drawn into the beak of a little creature like Phil, the juice can nourish the body of the insect from the time it hatches from an egg until it grows to be about a month old.

The juice in the grass stem which Phil drank would not have made very good bubbles just by itself; but by the time it had been sucked into Phil's mouth and passed out of an opening at his tail it was mixed with something from inside his body and was exactly right for bubbles. Phil did not make bubbles with his mouth. He made them with his tail. He would stick the tip of his tail out to the edge of the bubble house and, after getting some air, would draw it back and mix the air with the juice and make bubbles that way. The bubbles piled up somewhat as they do in the white of an egg when your mother whips it with an egg beater.

The next time you see a mass of white froth on a grass stem, you will know that there is a young insect inside making bubbles. Some people have not stopped to see what made such froth but have tried to guess without doing any real thinking. That is why it happens that there are silly names for the froth. In America some of these names are "cow-spit" and "frog-spit" and "snake-spit"; and in England one name is "cuckoo-spittle."

I am not going to tell you much about the size and shape of the bubble blowers that make the froth that is common in meadows and other places where grass grows tall; because you can easily look and see for yourself some day. It is perhaps enough to say that Phil was little and yellow and soft. Indeed his body was so tender that he needed cool moist bubbles next his skin to save him from the sunshine of hot dry weather.

Phil needed his house of bubbles all the time he was a baby insect; but suddenly one day, when he was about a month old, counting from the time he was hatched, he walked out of his air castle and never went back. From that day forth he did not blow another bubble.

The sun shone upon him but he did not seek shelter. The strong wind hit against him and he only clung the tighter to the swaying grass. If a hunting spider came near him, he jumped lightly to another stem. When a bird reached to grab him, he lifted his own tiny wings and sailed out of reach.

He could do these things because a great change had come to his body and he was now a grown insect. He was nearly one fifth of an inch long. His last wingless molted skin was beside the mass of bubbles that had once been his home; and his pretty air castle was now no more to him than his cast-off skin. He no longer needed to soak in a bubble bath. His skin was now tough enough so that the sun did not harm it. He was at last an active little creature. His hind legs were strong for jumping. His gray wings were whitish near the edges and had blackish lines for trimming.

Phil and Phyllis, many times larger than they really were.

One day when Phil was leaping among the grass stems and flying here and there, he met Phyllis; and they became mates. In time Phil was the father of a large family of eggs which Phyllis left, one in a place, in Holiday Meadow. She did not brood them. They were at the mercy of winter snows and freezing winds. Of course Phyllis must not be blamed for flying away from her eggs. That is the habit of her kind.

A good enough habit it proved to be, for one year from the day when Phil and Phyllis had hatched, their young ones broke their eggshells. Each of the numerous brothers and sisters began a solitary air castle. If you wish to know what went on in each little bubble house, you may read this story over again. Or, better yet, you may go into a meadow some day in June and find out for yourself.

CHAPTER VI

HAY DAY

TIMOTHY was a tuft of Herd's grass. He and several other tufts of long narrow thin flat leaves grew close together in a bunch. Besides these leaves Timothy had a slender straight stem about three feet tall. The base of this stem was shaped somewhat like a very little onion. This part was in the ground. At the other end of the stem were Timothy's many flowers crowded together in a spike-shaped tip.

In the field with Timothy were thousands of plants like him and altogether they were lovely to look at. When the breezes passed over them the tips of the grasses went down and then up like waves. As they touched one another in the wind they made pleasant murmuring sounds.

Timothy could not hear his own whispers or the lispings of his neighbors. He could not hear the tune of the little green musician who often clung to his stem and played.

The musician's name was a long Greek word which means *"I-dance-in-the-meadows."* He was a graceful creature with six jointed legs, the hind pair being very

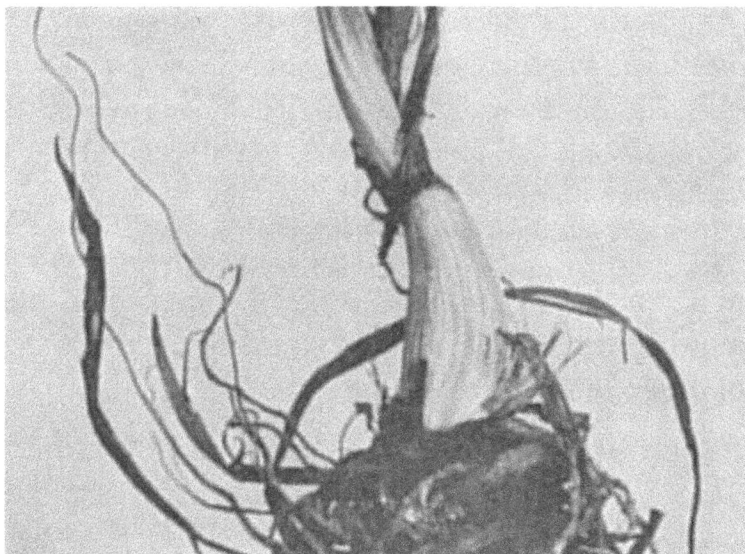

The stem of the Timothy grass is thickened at its base.

long and useful when he went skipping and hopping here and there. His green body was a little more than an inch long and his waving threadlike antennae were about two inches long. He had a neat brown stripe on top of his head. His tiny jaws moved sidewise, instead of up and down, and his manners when he ate were most dainty. When he was thirsty he drank dew drops from the tips of grass leaves. It was pleasant to see him.

His hind wings folded and unfolded in straight creases like fans. He used them in flying. His fore wings were long and narrow. Their edges overlapped a bit along the back and they covered and protected the more delicate hind wings when these were folded. Near its base each overlapping fore wing was thickened and ridged to form a musical instrument, for little *"I-dance-in-the-meadows"* played his tune by rubbing his wings together very rapidly.

There were short sharp notes like "zip-zip-zip!" in his music, and there were high-pitched and rather soft trills like "zreeeeeeeeee!" He played in the warm weather in the daytime and in the evening, but his cheeriest zips and trills were never heard by Timothy.

Timothy, indeed, could not hear even the loudest noise in the meadow. He did not know when the mowing machine clattered into the field and the racket of the cutting blades began.

But Dick and his cousin Anne heard the sounds though they were playing way down by the pond. "Hurrah!" cried Dick. "Hay day!" cried Anne. Then they both ran to the meadow as fast as they could go.

The cousins loved Holiday Meadow. It was a fragrant place with its clover and other sweet-scented blossoms. The notes of bumblebees and bobolinks and thousands of other musicians flooded it as full of pleasant sounds as a concert hall. And there were so many little creatures performing in the field that the children could not watch them all at the same time.

Anne had an especial liking for the Herd's grass. It grew so straight and was so thick and tall that she enjoyed walking among the stems. And when the Timothy heads were in full flower the lavender anthers, hanging from the blossoms, made the meadow lovely as if it were covered with a mist of color.

The children had many happy times in the meadow. Most exciting of all were the "hay days" when the men cut and raked the grass and then piled the dry hay on the big wagon and hauled it to the barn where they stowed

Jack was younger than Dick and Anne.

it to use in winter. Of course Dick and Anne tumbled on the hay stacks and rode on the loaded wagon; and sometimes they were permitted to help drive the horse that pulled the rake, after the grass was cut.

Anne, now, enjoyed the fun of haying as much as Dick did, though her first hay day had an unhappy beginning. That was during her first summer at Holiday Farm while she was a very little girl.

"Do you remember," asked Dick, "how you ran out in front of the horses and screamed until the man stopped the mowing machine?"

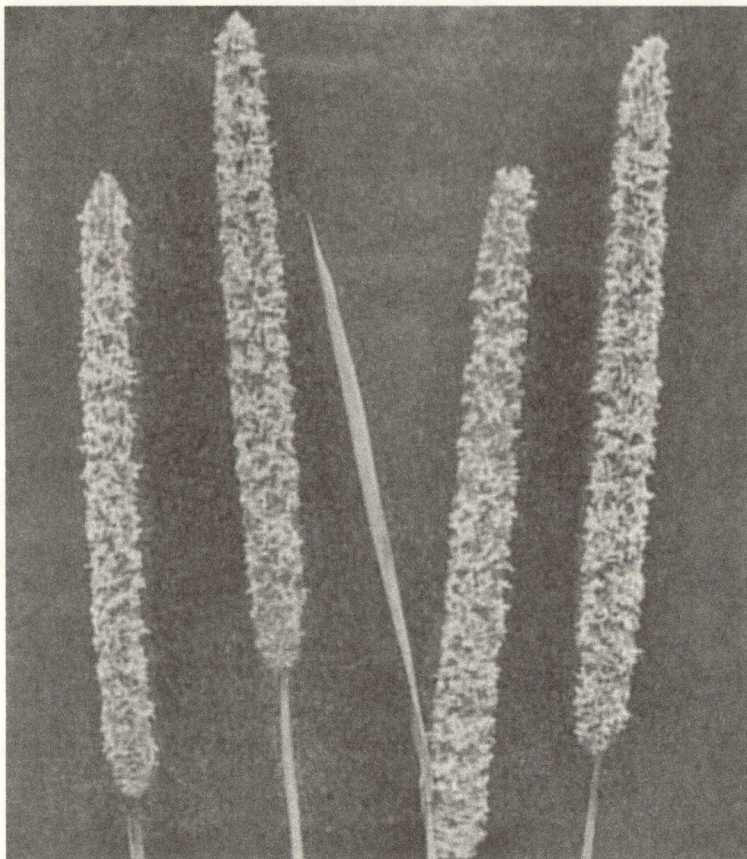

The Flowers of Timothy Grass

"Yes, I thought all the lovely Timothies were being hurt until Uncle David explained that they couldn't feel the cutting blades. You see, we had such good times playing hide-and-seek in the tall grass and talking to it and calling it 'Timothy' that I had a feeling that the tufts of grass were like people, I suppose. They seemed like our little playmates."

Anne touched a head of Herd's grass gently. "Even now," she said, "I wonder what sort of life this Timothy has. It grows year after year in the meadow and never sees the summer shadows when the fluffy clouds go over it. It never sees the spotted eggs the bobolink lays in the nest at its feet. It can't hear the crickets or the grasshoppers or the birds or the wind. It doesn't smell the clover or its own blossoms. It doesn't feel any pain when it is cut in two. And yet it is *alive*—as we are."

"Maybe it has some sort of feeling," said Dick, "while its stems are growing up into the light and its roots are pushing down through the dark ground; but I suppose no *person* can guess what it is like."

The cousins often told each other their thoughts about matters of this sort; but hay day was too exciting a time for long talks.

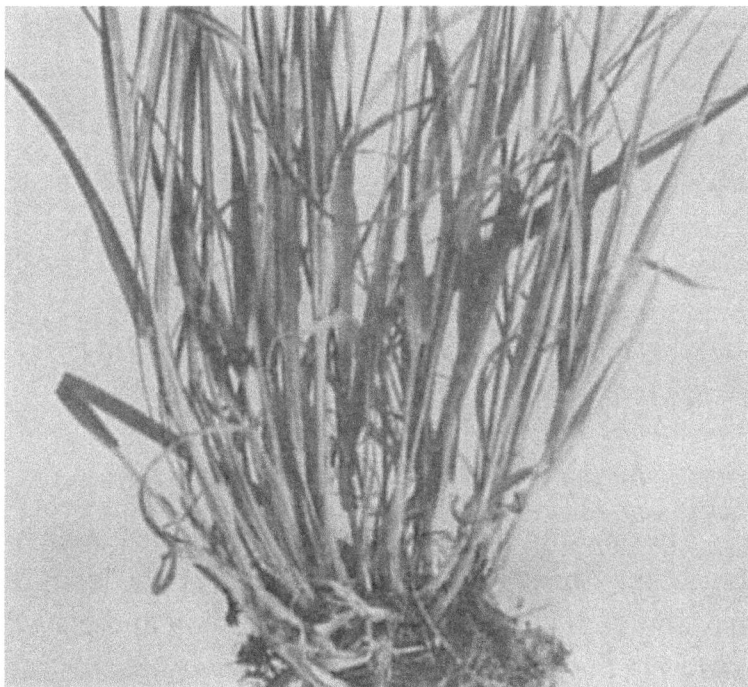

A Tuft of Timothy Grass

"Look!" exclaimed Anne. "You remember that bumblebee nest we found at the edge of the field among the golden rod? It was in the same spot where a mouse had a nest last year."

"That's so," said Dick. "John is driving the horses right towards it. We'd better run over and stop him in a hurry or he and the horses will be stung!"

The dry grass is ready to be taken to the barn.

The day after the grass was cut it was dry enough to be put into the barn. The children rode on the loads of hay and then climbed up into the hay-loft and played games in the fresh hay.

That evening Uncle David told Dick and Anne

about a hay day in England when he was a boy visiting there, with his father.

"When the grass was dry," he told them, "the hay-makers hauled it to the edge of the field. There they piled it carefully in big long stacks. Then men who knew how to make thatching came and covered each of the stacks with a sloping thatched roof of hay. The stacks were shaped like cottages and, together with some tall elms which stood near them, they were pleasant to remember—like a pretty picture."

The grass in England which is stored in neat thatched stacks is the same kind as that which Dick and Anne

In England hay is kept in neat stacks.

saw harvested in their uncle's meadow. Some people in England call it "Timothy grass" as we do. Others call it "cat's-tail" because of the shape of the blossom-spike.

After the grass in Holiday Meadow was cut, a party of crows came there for picnics. They were jolly noisy birds and had a merry time looking for insects in the stubble. Very early in the morning, before certain kinds of night cutworms had hidden themselves in the ground for the day, the crows went hunting for cutworms. Later, when the sun was bright, they had grasshopper hunts and amused themselves in other ways.

One day, not long after haying time, dull heavy clouds hung over Holiday Meadow and rain fell and

After the grass was cut it grew again.

soaked the ground. The grass plants found the moisture in the soil with their roots and began to grow new leaves. In a few weeks the field looked fresh and flourishing for the new leaves were high enough to hide the ends of the dry cut stubble.

Then Dick and Anne were permitted to take down the pasture bars and invite Daisy and the other cows into the meadow for a feast of fresh grass which was better than the trampled sod of the pasture.

When the cows had enjoyed the change for a week or two, they were put back behind their pasture bars. The grass in the meadow needed a chance to grow before frosts came so that it could store up strength in its underground stems and be in good condition to stand the cold weather.

One morning the frost showed white and heavy on the grass blades, and after that the plants rested for several months. In time the snow fell on the field and tucked the thousands of sleeping Timothies under a soft thick blanket, for winter days and nights.

And not a Timothy of them all knew what had happened to him!

The iris made blue reflections in the water.

CHAPTER VII

STAR NOSE

Holiday Meadow stretches from its high dry part, where it touches Holiday Hill, to a low swamp where it slopes down to Holiday Stream.

In the bank of the stream there is a round hole, the opening from a long tunnel. The water splashes against the hole and, during rainy weather, rises and covers it. The hole is not large enough for a rat to enter. It is larger than a mouse would need.

Some wild iris plants grow beside the hole and their lovely blue June and July flowers are reflected in the water.

Sedges and rushes are near enough so that the tips of some of their long narrow grass-like green leaves touch the iris. Their brown worn-out last year's leaves lie tangled on the ground like a rough mat. Beyond the iris and sedges the fluffy white tops of the cotton grass are stirred by the breezes.

And in August the swampy place is bright with yellow golden-rod and soft with rose-purple Joe-Pye Weed.

The Fluffy White Tops of the Cotton Grass

The hole in the bank of the stream was not always empty. Often a furry little animal poked her head out of it and dipped her queer snout into the water. The end of her nose was shaped somewhat like two star-fishes pressed together, because it was circled with twenty-two slender feelers that pointed outward. This quaint animal was a star-nosed mole.

Sometimes little Star Nose came out of the hole and swam in the water. Sometimes she ran on top of the ground under the mat of brown sedge leaves. Indeed, she had a path under the sedge leaves. The path was rather smooth and firm where her feet and body had pressed against it. It had an arched roof where her back had pushed up against the brown fibers while she ran along the trail. There were places where the roof had been torn by the hard feet of Daisy, the cow, when she was out of the pasture and came down to the stream to drink.

But, even when Star Nose ran along that part of the path where the roof was gone, it is likely that she never saw the white tips of the cotton grass swaying in the wind or the yellow blossoms of the golden-rod or the rose-purple Joe-Pye flowers.

The Front Part of a Star-Nosed Mole

The Rose-Purple Blossoms of Joe-Pye Weed

And, when she drank at the hole by the stream, she probably saw neither the blue iris blossoms above her head nor their blue reflections in the water below her funny nose. She may not have known what the experience would be like to see the shape or the color of anything in the world.

You need not feel sorry for Star Nose. You need not pity her because her tiny eyes were so covered by fur that she could, perhaps, sense no more than a difference between the brightness of the sunshine, where it touched the water near her drinking hole, and the darkness of her deepest underground trails. It was enough for her to feel and hear and smell and taste.

Star Nose was a hunter. She had hunted day and night ever since she was old enough to follow the hunting paths. Of course she rested now and then, but her recesses from hunting were short because she was so well and strong that she seemed never to be really tired.

While some of Star Nose's hunting paths were above ground, covered by old brown matted swamp leaves, most of them were underground tunnels that went here and there through the soil. For long distances these trails lay just under the sod of the meadow but in many places they were several feet deep in the ground.

Every time Star Nose passed along one of the paths her feet, pressing against the floor, made it a bit more firm; and her fur, where it touched the sides, brushed them a bit more smooth.

The more Star Nose ran the hungrier she became; and the more she ate the more she felt like running. So her days and nights were busy—hunting and eating. Almost as soon as she had eaten her breakfast she was ready to hunt for a luncheon and by the time one luncheon was over she was in the mood to scurry off for another. That is the sort of lively hunter Star Nose was!

For many of her meals she ate insects. There was a flavor about white-grubs that she relished. White-grubs, as perhaps you know, hatch from the eggs that May-beetles lay. Their bodies are plump and curled and they lie on their backs in the ground while they reach up and chew the roots of grasses or other plants. Some years there were thousands and thousands of white-grubs in the meadow, so many, indeed, that had it not been for Star Nose and the other moles much of the grass would have died for lack of roots.

This kind of mole does not have a star nose.

There was a taste about cutworms that pleased Star Nose. Cutworms, as you may have heard, hatch from the eggs that owlet-moths lay. There are many kinds of these hairless caterpillars that spend their days resting in the ground and their nights nibbling parts of meadow or garden plants. If it were not for moles, cutworms would do much more harm to wild and cultivated plants because then there would be so many more of them.

Star Nose enjoyed many a dinner of wireworms. Wireworms hatch from the eggs of click-beetles (or snapping-beetles). They live in the ground and eat the roots of grasses and certain other plants. If it had not been for Star Nose and others of her kind, the loads of Timothy grass would not have been as large as they were on hay day.

It would take too many pages for the full bill-of-fare of Star Nose. Perhaps enough has been said to suggest that many of the plants of Holiday Meadow were better off because Star Nose lived and hunted there. But at least one more article of the mole's diet should be mentioned. She liked to eat earthworms.

Earthworms, of course, hatch from earthworm eggs and grow only from little earthworms to big earthworms and never change into anything else whatever. They make their homes in the ground although they come out of their holes at night and crawl about in the dark. They need moisture. In rainy weather, when the ground is wet, they stay near the surface; but during drought they go deeper into the soil until they reach damp earth. They need, also, to escape getting too cold so they go below frost for the winter.

It is largely because of earthworms that some of the hunting paths of the moles are deep in the ground. The hunters follow their game—up when the earth is moist and down when the soil is dry or very cold.

Star Nose, herself, did not so much mind the cold. Sometimes, indeed, she swam in the stream even after the surface of the water was covered with ice. Sometimes, on a winter day, she dug up through the snow that lay on the meadow.

Her thick coat was warm. The fine soft hairs were close together and they stood straight on end. She was in no danger of having her fur rubbed the wrong way for it looked the same whether it was stroked up from the tail or down from the head.

During most of the year Star Nose hunted alone and paid little attention to other moles when she chanced to meet them at the crossings of the hunting paths. But in the spring there were four little moles who received her devoted care. They were her baby sons and daughters, so of course she did not neglect them.

She had a comfortable den for them in a dry place under a stump in the hedgerow. The hedge was at one side of the meadow and even when the swampy land near the stream was flooded in spring, the ground about the hedge was well drained and above water level.

Star Nose's den under the stump was about a foot deep in the ground. She had put a ball of fine grass in the den and in this soft round nest the four little moles had their bed.

At first the babies were naked and fat and wrinkled and pink and helpless. They could not hunt and for a while their only food was their mother's milk. This agreed with them so well that they grew rapidly. Before they were many weeks old they were full-sized moles and looked like their mother and father.

Their thick soft velvety fur coats were of a dark color that seemed almost too black to be gray and almost too gray to be black. Their noses were star-shaped. And they had most wonderful hands.

Of course all the underground hunting paths and highways and dens of the moles must first be dug before they can be used. And for this digging moles need no other shovels than their paddle-shaped hands.

*   *   *   *   *

Suppose you should try to dig with your hands long tunnels in the ground big enough so that you could crawl through them! Would not your fingers soon become tired and sore? And even if your hands were strong enough for so rough a task, would not the dirt come tumbling into your eyes and your ears? Would you not be more comfortable with undeveloped eyes covered over with fur with no dirt getting into them and making them ache? And, if you had tunnels to dig day after day, would you not prefer to have no big ear-flaps to catch the dirt—even if you could not hear quite so well without them?

*   *   *   *   *

The sort of digging that would be impossible for an animal whose body is not fitted for such work is as natural as swimming for a mole. Indeed, when the soil is moist and soft and a mole digs close to the sod, he moves through the dirt as if he were swimming with strong slow strokes. He puts his large powerful hands forward, palms outward, until the tips of his claws touch in front of his nose. Then he thrusts his hands outward and backward, pushing the soil aside and forcing his body ahead. The damp soil close to the sod is loose enough so that he does not need to bring any of it to the surface to get it out of his way. He just pushes it aside and packs it firmly as he "swims" through the ground.

But when a mole digs his deep runways where the soil is not loose enough to be pushed aside in this manner, he brings earth, which he digs from his tunnel, to the surface of the ground and throws it outside in a heap.

After the four young moles were old enough to do their own hunting and digging, each one ran off alone along the hunting trails. If one of the sons met his mother, Star Nose, at some crossing, he did not tease her to bring him a white-grub for dinner. If one of the daughters met her father, Moldwarp,[1] she did not beg him to show her where the grasshopper eggs were thickest. If one of them met a grandmother or grandfather or uncle or aunt or cousin, the relatives did not spend time in visiting. For a mole is a natural hunter. He would rather hunt than play.

So, even when Holiday Meadow looks very quiet indeed, you may know that quaint little creatures of the underways are scurrying here and there along old hunting paths or busily digging new ones. And if you ever expect to see one of these busy creatures throwing earth in a tiny hill, outside his hole you will need to "tread softly that the blind mole may not hear a foot fall" or feel the ground tremble as you step.

---

[1]*Moldwarp* is an old name for mole. The word means "dust thrower" or "earth thrower."

CHAPTER VIII

THE ADVENTURES OF
A MEADOW CATERPILLAR

CTENUCHA[2] had her first adventure while she was young. She was, indeed, so very young that she was still living inside an eggshell when things began to happen.

The eggshell which was her first home was shaped like a ball, except that one side was flat. The flat side was fastened to a blade of grass. The egg was so small that it would have taken more than twenty like it, resting side by side, to make a row an inch long. There were nearly two hundred such eggs in rows on grass blades near the egg in which she lived. Inside of each of these was a brother or sister of Ctenucha's.

After she had lived for ten days in the egg, it changed color. It had been yellow at first, as yellow as honey. On the eleventh day the egg looked gray. The shell itself was not gray. It was really as white as a pearl. It looked gray because something inside had turned dark and was pressing against the shell. The dark thing was Ctenucha's head.

[2] *"Ctenucha"* is a Greek name. You speak it as if it were spelled "Tenuka."

69

The next day the dark head showed even more plainly through the thin shell. It was about this time that little Ctenucha began to move her jaws in a hungry way. It is not unpleasant to be hungry if there is good food to eat, and the tiny caterpillar liked eggshell. She scraped and scraped against the shell for hours until at last she made a hole in it. There was no reason then why she could not have crept through the hole, except that she was so hungry for eggshell that she ate her way out instead. After a time she was no longer inside the shell but most of the shell was inside of her.

That was Ctenucha's first adventure, eating her way into a world of sunshine. You need not be surprised to learn that a creature who began life so strangely should do other queer things from time to time. That is, they seem odd to us, though all Ctenucha really did was to live a natural caterpillar life. If you wish to see for yourself how she acted, you need only find an egg like hers and watch from the time the baby insect eats its eggshell until its last adventure.

Ctenucha had sixteen feet. Three pairs of them were on jointed legs near her head. These she did not use much in walking. She held them somewhat like hands at each side of her food when she was eating. She crept with the other five pairs, soft clinging feet with which she could hold firmly to the thin edge of grass.

She did not need to learn to creep, and it was well for her that she could travel at once; for, soon after she had finished her breakfast of eggshell, she was ready for dinner. Perhaps it was the smell of growing grass that made her hungry, for as soon as she came to a tender leaf she began to nibble it. From the moment she first tasted grass she seemed contented with that sort of food; and, as long as she was a caterpillar, she sought no other kind. Her journeys to the market took her no farther than from one grass plant to another; and some days she ate so steadily that it would be hard to tell when her breakfast ended and her supper began.

After eating busily for several days, she stopped to rest. She was forced to stop because she had grown so fast that her skin could not hold any more body. When she was in that sort of fix she pulled herself out of her skin, but that took time.

She rested quietly until the tight skin ripped back of her head. Then she crept out of it, leaving the skin— old skull and all—lying on the grass. She did not need it any longer because a new coat of skin had grown to take its place. Now she could again eat grass until this new coat should in its turn become too tight and need to be discarded.

That is the way Ctenucha passed the days until fall—eating, growing, resting, molting. Every time she molted she had a different-looking skin. She changed her coat for a bigger and prettier one each time. Her first little coat had been pale yellow with tiny black dots from each of which grew a few dark hairs. Each new coat had more hairs than the one before. The garment she was wearing when cold weather came had a row of black hairs down the middle of the back and a stripe of yellow hairs on each side.

Ctenucha's home was in Holiday Meadow where, during the cold winter, the grass stops growing and the ground is covered deeply with snow.

Some animals in the north must live all winter without eating. Bats and bears and woodchucks and skunks and frogs and earthworms and many insects can do this. All these animals that live without eating during the winter manage in much the same way. Each seeks a comfortable place and goes to sleep. That is what Ctenucha did. She slept while the weather was cold.

Her winter adventure was a nap. But her sleep was not so sound as that of some of the other dozing animals. When the weather was warm enough, as perhaps during a January thaw, she wakened and went for a walk. Dick and Anne, who were tramping across the fields on their snowshoes one mild day, saw a black-and-yellow creature hurrying over the snow and they called it a "winter caterpillar" and wondered where it was going.

After fasting all winter, Ctenucha was very hungry in the spring. As soon as the grass began to grow she ate greedily. The coat in which she had slept was no longer pretty. The yellow hairs had faded until they were the color of old straw, and the black tufts had become dingy. She could not change this garment for a better one until she was plump enough to molt; but by the middle of April she had eaten so many tender grass blades that she could not swallow another mouthful. It was time for her spring molting to take place at last.

She then crept to a bit of stubble and spun a thin

mat of silk upon a dry stem. She tangled the hooks of her ten creeping feet among the threads of the mat and rested quietly with her head down. After a while she pulled her head out of her old skull and she then looked as if she had a swollen neck. The new head inside the old skin pressed so hard that at last the skin tore at the "collar" and Ctenucha's head popped through the hole. She pulled her six jointed legs and her ten creeping feet out of their old stockings and crept forth like a new creature. She left her old coat lying on her molting-mat on the stubble and went in search of fresh grass. She was very hungry again.

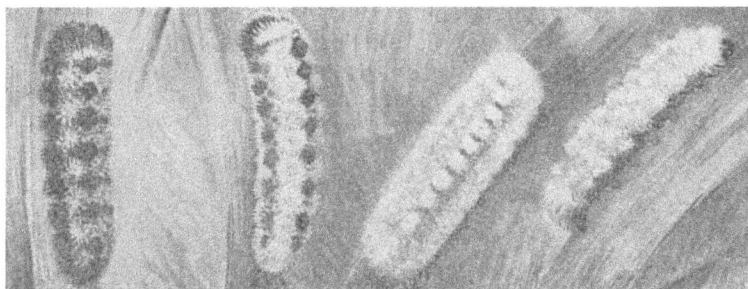

Patterns in the Coats Worn by Ctenucha Caterpillars

The winter coat she had just molted had, as you may remember, a row of black tufts down the middle of the back. There were more than one thousand caterpillars of the same kind in the meadow where she lived; and every one of them wore a winter coat like hers, with black tufts in a row down the back. All these thousand and more caterpillars molted their winter coats in the spring, after they had eaten grass for some time. Some of the new spring coats had black tufts on the back and some of them had white tufts. Of course the caterpillars could not choose which color of tufts they would have. Each one had the kind that grew, just as you have dark hair or light hair without choosing.

Ctenucha's spring coat had a row of white tufts bordered on each side by a soft yellow stripe. Her ten creeping feet were red—not bright red but a soft dark shade. Her head was the same pretty color as her feet, except her face which was black. If, some spring day, you chance to meet a creature like her, with a black and red skin and a yellow and white coat, you will doubtless be glad to see so good-looking a caterpillar.

Fine as the new spring coat was it did not last long; for one day Ctenucha pulled the hair out of it and then she was as queer as a hen, without any feathers.

The day she pulled out her hair was the time of one of her greatest adventures—the day she made her cocoon. I like to remember that day because she wove a basket-like cocoon without making one mistake; although she had never made a cocoon before and there was no one to show her how to do it.

After Ctenucha had taken the last bite of grass she was ever to swallow, she sought a piece of bent stubble and crept to the under side of it. Clinging to the dry stem, back down, she began to spin. Perhaps you know that a caterpillar has silk glands in its body where liquid silk is made. When a caterpillar is ready to spin, the silk drools out of an opening through the lower lip and, when it touches the air, it is stiffened into thread.

Ctenucha had spun silk before. She had made a mat of silk in which to tangle the hooks of her creeping feet while she molted. The molting-mat held her old skin steady while she pulled herself out of it. But to make silk enough to cover her whole body was quite a different task.

First she spun a strip of silk about as long as her body upon the lower edge of the stubble. She clung to this with her creeping feet while she made the rest of her cocoon. When she was spinning she used her jointed feet somewhat like little hands to guide the thread and to help shape the cocoon. She wove the edges down at each side and each end until they nearly met at the middle and then she joined the edges.

Some caterpillars weave their cocoons entirely of silk, but Ctenucha did not. She used hair also, making a kind of haircloth cocoon; and the hair that she used she pulled out of her coat. First she would add some silk to the edge of the cocoon, and then she would reach her head back and grasp a mouthful of hair close to her skin and pull it out. It came out quickly as if it were loose. I do not think the jerk hurt her. She would tuck the mouthful of hair endwise into the silk she had just spun. Then she would spin more silk in which to tuck the next mouthful of hair which she pulled out.

She worked without wasting any time or any motions. When she was spinning the left side of the cocoon, she reached to her left side and pulled hair from that part of her coat. By pulling hair that was nearest the place she was spinning, she saved time and strength. She did not weave in a nervous quick way. She wove slowly and steadily and she did not stop to rest until the cocoon was quite completed.

Haircloth cocoons woven by Ctenucha caterpillars, with a pupa, which is the stage between a caterpillar and a moth.

By the time Ctenucha's cocoon was finished, her body was stripped of its hair. She had just enough hair for the cloth of her cocoon. Do you not think that it is wonderful that she could weave that perfect little basket-like cocoon the first time she tried? No one to show her how! Not stopping until it was finished! Measuring out her hair so that there was enough for the cocoon and none to spare!

It seems fitting that she should have a marvelous

cocoon, for remarkable events occurred inside it. In fact, two of her best adventures took place in her cocoon.

When her weaving was over, Ctenucha lay quivering with the changes that were taking place in her body. After a day or so of waiting, her caterpillar skin ripped down the middle of the back far enough so that she could squirm out of it. She looked queer while she was doing this, for she was not a caterpillar any longer. She was, instead, a soft wriggling object with six legs (much longer than any she had had before), four wing-pads that flopped a very little, a long straight quivering tongue, and two feelers. Legs, wing-pads, tongue, and feelers all moved feebly for a minute or two and then they became glued fast to her body by the fluid that had helped loosen the old caterpillar skin. When the air inside the cocoon touched this fluid it hardened it into a sort of glue.

Ctenucha was a caterpillar no longer. She had changed into a pupa. When she first became a pupa, she was bright red with a row of cream-colored spots down her back, but she soon turned dark brown all over and was so shiny that she looked as if she were covered with varnish. At the tail-end of the pupa there were some tiny hooks that caught into the silk of the cocoon.

First she had been an egg, and then a caterpillar, and then a pupa. What next would she be? Next she would be a moth; but not until she had lain waiting, as a pupa, for sixteen days. During that time her little body underwent its last great change.

Then the shiny brown skin cracked open and she

came out of it. The hooks on the end of the pupa-case held it steady while she pulled herself free. She pushed her way through one end of the cocoon and waited for her wings to expand and grow strong.

Ctenucha was at last a moth, a full-grown insect with wings; and the adventures that lay ahead of her were quite different from those of her caterpillar days.

Full-Grown Ctenuchas

I cannot tell you whether she had a better time after she came out of the cocoon than she did before she wove herself inside of it. I can only say that she had acted as if she were a contented caterpillar while she was nibbling her first breakfast of eggshell, while she was munching her many dinners of grass, and while she was weaving her wonderful cocoon. After she became a moth, she still acted as if it gave her pleasure to be alive and in motion.

Most kinds of moths fly only at night, but Ctenucha flew during the sunlight hours. She visited clover, the spreading dogbane, meadow sweet, viburnum, and other flowers. She carried her long tongue coiled tight like a watch-spring while she was flying; but when she reached a flower, she straightened her tongue and put the tip of it into the tube of the blossom and sipped the sweet nectar she found there.

Ctenucha visited the flowers for nectar.

She drank dew, too, feeling along the grass blades with the tip of her tongue and sipping the dewdrops as she did nectar. Sometimes she went to bushes and trees where there were colonies of aphids and drank the sweet liquid, called honeydew, that aphids drop from their bodies.

It was not easy to see her colors when she was flying, but while she was feeding at a flower it was possible to look closely. Her fore wings were queerly colored. Sometimes they looked rusty black or brown and sometimes bronze or purple or green. Like "changeable silk" their colors were different when they were turned in different ways toward the light. Her hind wings were bluish black or blackish blue. All four of her wings were narrowly edged with white. Her body was glistening peacock blue with a dash of bright orange just behind her head. Her head was orange-colored, too, except the middle of her face which was blue, and her feelers and mouth parts which were black.

However pleasant she may have found the flowers, she did not spend all her time among them. She had another adventure of much importance. There were her eggs, nearly two hundred of them, that needed to be glued to grass blades. Even the sweet taste of nectar or honeydew did not tempt her to neglect her eggs. She put them in rows, close together, sometimes more than twenty on a single leaf of grass.

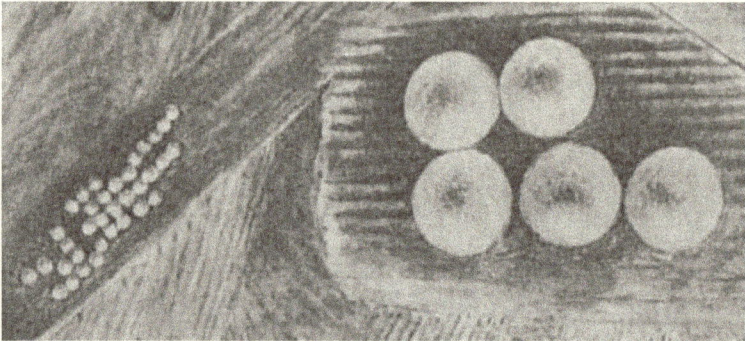

Ctenucha's Eggs. Those on the right, greatly enlarged.

Like the one in which she herself had started life, they were yellow as honey and round except for one flat side. And they were tiny, but not too tiny to hold the promise of many adventures; for inside of each egg was a speck of life that could grow to be a caterpillar, then a pupa, and then a moth.

All the time that I have been telling you about the adventures of Ctenucha, I have been wishing that you might have an adventure of your own. I have been wishing that you might see an egg like one of Ctenucha's hatch; or notice such a caterpillar at molting time; or watch one weave a cocoon; or find a moth whose body is glistening blue trimmed with bright orange, and whose wings have queer changing colors. Perhaps my wish for your adventure may come true. Wishes often do.

The snow buntings perched on a row of trees near the house.

CHAPTER IX

SNOWFLAKES

A DECEMBER storm was blowing across Holiday Meadow. Snow drifted with the wind, the flakes fluttering over the field like flocks of tiny birds.

Dick and Anne, who were trudging toward a farm house, paused to watch the falling snow. They pushed their backs against the wind to keep from losing foothold. Their coats flapped at their sides like tugging sails.

Suddenly some of the distant flakes of snow seemed to grow larger and to move on white wings before the driving wind. The cousins blinked in surprise and looked again and saw, indeed, a flock of birds drifting with the snow. They were flying low, only a few feet from the ground.

A moment before there had been no sounds except those of the storm as it swirled against the meadow weeds. Now thin twittery notes mingled with the rough voice of the wind, making quaint winter music.

The two looked at each other and smiled. "The snowflakes have come," said Anne. "It is early in the season for them, too; for we do not always see them in December, do we?"

"No," said Dick, "the snow must be so deep farther north that they could not wait any longer for their visit to us. They have probably been staying near the coast for some time before they came here."

In another minute the birds were out of sight and hearing. They had made the storm seem live and beautiful. "The darlings!" said one of the children. "They did not fight the wind. They flew with it as if they were a part of the storm."

Every year Dick and Anne watched for the snow-flakes, or snow buntings as they are also called, that come from their arctic home to a more temperate climate for the winter and sometimes for the early spring.

It probably is not the cold that sends them southward for they are hardy birds and thrive in zero weather, or colder, if they can find food enough for their hearty appetites. But when the seedy tops of the arctic plants have become buried in snow, these birds seek fields where the snow is not so deep. Their southward winter flight depends more on the depth of the snow than on the coldness of the weather; and it takes place much earlier some years than others.

For weeks the flock of snow buntings that had flown past Dick and Anne in the storm visited the fields where for miles in all directions there was plenty of food. During that December even short plants stood above the snow that thinly covered the ground. Early in January the snow became deep enough to hide the clover heads and the grasses.

The tall sedges were bowed with snow.

Later in the month the cold white fluff was piled high against the stems of wild carrot, or Queen Anne's lace, the cup-shaped heads of which still held their seeds above the drifts. Then one night about the first of February there came a fall of snow that buried the tallest of the Queen Anne's lace plants. Even the mullein stalks held only the highest of their seed-pods in sight.

Early the next morning when the cousins saw what had happened, Dick said, "The snowflakes will be hungry to-day. We'd better get their picnic ground ready for them."

The snow covered all the plants except the tall ones.

So the children put on their snowshoes and trampled back and forth and around and around in the yard south of the house until they had packed the snow rather hard and firm. Then they brought hay from the barn and scattered it over the packed snow and tramped that down, too, so that it would not blow away in the wind. The hay on the snow made a dark place that looked at a distance like bare ground.

When hungry birds see such places they come to hunt for seeds. There were some grass seeds among the dry hay but not enough for a real bird picnic. So the cousins brought out some clover seeds and poured them in several heaps near the hay.

The snow buntings had spent the stormy night several miles away in some rather sheltered spot. That morning, when they were ready for breakfast, they flew high overhead and looked down for signs of food. As far as they could see, the fields were white. So they flew on and on. The farther they flew the hungrier they became.

Then suddenly a small flock of the buntings saw a dark place in a dooryard not far from Holiday Meadow. It looked like bare ground. Perhaps there would be seeds there! They flew lower and lower and alighted near the edge of the meadow. They waited and watched the tempting dark place on the ground. It was close to a house and they felt timid. But most of all they felt hungry and there was nothing for them to eat on the white bare field.

The bravest of them flew a little way toward the spot, going low—only a few feet above the snow. Then he stopped flying and ran a while. He could not run very fast for his feet sank into the soft new snow and he had to wade. While he was wading the rest of the flock flew and caught up with him one by one. So wading and flying they approached the dooryard.

At last the bravest of the flock again flew ahead and this time alighted on some trampled hay beside a little heap of clover seeds. He began to eat. He was happy. He twittered as he ate. His comrades heard him twittering and came quickly to the feast. Soon they were all there—all eating seeds and all twittering.

The birds twittered while they ate.

The boy and girl watched them from inside the window. They stood quietly so that no motion should frighten the birds.

"The snowflakes have found their picnic," whispered Dick. "There are only twelve of them," said Anne wistfully, "I wish more would come."

Anne had her wish. The next day thirty buntings came to their picnic grounds and before a week had passed the flock numbered more than sixty.

After every storm, the children hurried out to tramp down more hay and heap seeds on the snow. Sometimes it snowed steadily all day and then they scattered fresh hay and put out new seeds about once an hour so that there would always be something for the birds to find.

The snow covered so many of the seeds and the large flock of birds ate so many more that it was not long before the clover seeds were gone. Neighbors gave the cousins leftover garden seeds but these would not last many days either. So Dick ordered a large sack of cracked grain from the store—a sort that is ground fine for very young chickens. This they mixed with their seeds and the buntings twittered as cheerfully while they were eating their new kind of food as if it had dropped from the seedy tops of meadow weeds.

Every now and then other snow buntings found their way to the picnic ground and by the first day of March there were more than one hundred in the flock.

The snow buntings found their picnic ground.

Among all these buntings there were no two that looked exactly alike. They were all pure white on the under parts of their wings and bodies. They all had rusty brown feathers and black ones on their sides and backs. But some had more white feathers and some had more brown ones and some had more black ones. The feather coat of each bird was thus a little different from all the others. Most of the birds had brown collars but these were of different shapes, some meeting in front and the edges of some not quite coming together, some being broad and some being narrow.

The heads of most of the buntings were bright brown on top. Only two birds in the flock had no brown feathers at all on their heads and necks. The children called these two birds the "white-headed snowflakes."

No two snow buntings were just alike.

The white-headed snowflakes did not often feed at the same pile of seeds. When they did so they stood at opposite sides. If another bunting came very near, one of the white-headed birds would spread his feet wide apart and make a sudden jumping motion toward the newcomer and scare it away.

Usually most of the birds in the flock were sociable and happy while they ate and their mealtime twitter was cheerful to hear. It seemed surprising that they could pick up their food so quickly and chatter so fast at the same time.

During a storm, however, when the snow began to cover the food, the birds became anxious. Then each one that found a little heap of seeds guarded it and tried to keep other birds away.

At first Dick and Anne thought the buntings were rather mean and stingy when they would not share such food with their comrades. But the more they watched the birds and thought about their ways, the more it seemed to them that the habits of the flock were rather good ones—for wild birds to have. For each bird that was driven away would be so hungry that it would try its very best to find some food for itself. So, in the end, all the birds were better fed than they could have been if they had all eaten at a few places and let the rest of the seeds become covered too deeply in the snow to be found.

Such habits would, of course, work the same way with hungry buntings that were feeding on weed seeds in a meadow. No bird could be lazy and take what another had found. Each one must be busy and find its own seeds. So all the birds in the flock would be able to take care of themselves. Perhaps that is one of the reasons why buntings are so strong and well during the cold winter weather.

Dick and Anne often watched one or another of the buntings hunt in the snow for seeds. It would put its bill down into the fresh snow and then jerk its head from side to side, throwing the snow to right and left until more and more food was uncovered.

All the buntings had the same way of shoveling snow with their bills by swinging their heads quickly from side to side; but certain other winter birds that also visited the picnic ground did not do this when they were hunting in the snow.

One day Anne chanced to look out of the window while the snow was falling fast and only a little seed remained in sight. One redpoll, one junco, and one bunting were feeding not far from one another.

The bunting was, of course, throwing the soft snow from side to side with its bill. The redpoll put its bill down directly in front of it and picked up what it could reach in that way. The junco scratched the snow in all directions—scratched with both feet, scattering the seeds widely, Some of them were thrown near the redpoll and the bunting and were eaten by these birds before the junco could pick them up himself.

The table-manners of these three birds were so amusing that Anne chuckled as she watched them.

The first day the buntings visited their picnic grounds they flew back across the field far from the yard every time they were frightened. Before long, however, they became less timid and began to perch in the trees near the house. There was a row of oak, maple, and elm

The snowflakes flew to the tree-tops.

trees along one side of the driveway. The buntings used all these trees, but most of all the tall elm which was not near the main road that passed the house.

If a heavy truck went along the road while the buntings were on the ground eating their seeds, or if they were startled by other moving or noisy objects, they flew to the topmost branches of this big elm. There they waited and seemed to feel as safe as if they had flown far across the meadow. When all was quiet again they would drift from the tree down to the ground.

These flights from the ground to the tree and down again took place many times a day. Dick and Anne never tired of watching the birds come down and counting them as they came. Usually the first bird to leave the tree would utter a sharp "Zurk" just as he started. After him, others would drift down one by one. Then as they began to chatter contentedly over the picnic seeds, the others would join them a few at a time.

If a strong wind was blowing, the birds would turn to face it just before reaching the ground, and then they would land with what seemed to be one shift of their wings. When there was no wind they fluttered their wings in a hovering motion while alighting.

Sometimes they floated from the topmost twigs directly to the ground in long slanting flight like flakes of drifting snow. But usually they dropped from the high branches to lower ones and then to those still lower, thus coming to the picnic ground in several short flights.

When Dick and Anne first noticed the buntings in the trees, they were surprised; for they were used to seeing them only in meadows and other open fields. Then, too, they had read in their bird books that snowflakes are ground birds, rarely perching in trees.

There are plenty of reasons, indeed, why these birds spend most of their time on the ground. In summer they nest in far northern treeless places. In winter they seek the seedy tops of grass and other plants of the fields. It is thus natural for them to run along the ground and walk on top of the snow.

Nevertheless snow buntings belong to the large order of perching birds; and, like their relatives the sparrows and finches, they can be comfortable and happy in trees. Doubtless the only reason why these birds do not rest on the twigs of trees more often is that usually trees are not near their feeding places.

However, Dick and Anne were now used to seeing the snow buntings in the tall trees of their yard for this was the third winter the cousins had kept their picnic ground ready for them.

The children belonged to a bird club which met once a month in the nearest city. Many of the members of the club had never seen snow buntings near at hand or heard them sing. So in March Dick and Anne gave a number of "snowflake parties" to which they invited their friends, four or five at a time. They served each time a simple "afternoon tea" sort of luncheon; and while the bird club guests were having their refreshments near the window inside the house, the buntings came down to their picnic served on the snow outside.

Then when the birds flew up to the tall elm near the back door, the tea party guests would tiptoe quietly into the back entry and stand by the open door to hear the sweet tinkling voices of the bunting chorus.

That March the voices of the buntings were the first morning sounds Dick and Anne heard through the open windows of their bedrooms. The children looked at their watches each morning when they heard the buntings and kept records in their notebooks.

Their favorite record was that of March the fourth. On that morning they heard the chattering calls of the buntings as they were flying toward the elm tree at just half past five. The cousins put on their warm robes and slippers and watched from the window. A large flock of the twittering birds settled on the high twigs of the elm.

Ten minutes later, one of the birds called "Zurk" and flew down to the picnic ground. The moon was bright in the sky at the time and Dick and Anne could see the birds against the snow as they drifted from the tree to the ground. Thirty went down, one at a time, and there were still many left twittering in the tree. Later, when it was lighter, the cousins counted eighty-four in the morning flock.

That day the time of sunrise was at twelve minutes past six, so you see the birds had come nearly three-quarters of an hour before sunrise.

Most of the time that month from sunrise or before to sunset or later, there were snow buntings on the picnic ground or in the elm tree. They took short flights to other places and the size of the flock varied from time to time. Some days as many as one hundred were there part of the time and some days the most that came were about twenty or thirty.

After the middle of March there was a change in the bunting chorus. Above the tinkling twitter, trills could be heard. Some of the trills were faltering and broken as if they came from birds that had never trilled before. Some were long and steady as if sung by birds that had trilled during other Marches. Each day the trilling became more clear and sure. It was never loud music and the faint tones could be heard only a little way; but before the end of March the full chorus had become wonderfully sweet.

Spring had touched the voices of the snow buntings! And spring was touching their wings! The flock was becoming smaller. Early in April the last of the buntings ate a farewell luncheon.

Under the high sun the snow on the fields had settled until the plant tops and stems were in plain sight. There was a seedy path from Holiday Meadow leading toward the north.

Northward Ho! the snow buntings were gone.

And later, when the meadowlarks that had spent their winter farther south were nesting in Holiday Meadow, Dick and Anne liked to think, too, of the snowflakes, far to the north, happy and busy with their grass-and-deer-hair nests in some sunny Arctic field.

CHAPTER X

THE SILK FUNNEL

AGALENA[3] had no backbone; but she was not a cripple. She could do much that no animal with a backbone can do. She had eight eyes. She had two more legs than an insect, and an insect has six legs. Her home was a web of silk. Yes, I am sure you have guessed, by this time, that Agalena was a spider.

Agalena and her many brothers and sisters spent the winter together in an egg-sac. The egg-sac was under the bark of an old stump. It was rather flat and it was protected by a sheet of silk.

A silk sheet does not seem a very warm covering for nights when the weather was so cold that the mercury in the thermometer went down to the zero mark. However, spider eggs keep well in cold storage when they are in a fairly dry place. If the baby spiders, still in their eggshells, were chilled during the winter it did them no harm. In early spring they hatched. Later, one warm day, Agalena ran off on her eight little legs and found a house lot for her home.

[3] *Ag-a-le´-na* is a name for certain spiders. The word means "without calmness" or "restless." It is also spelled *Agelena*.

The stump under the bark of which she, while an egg, had spent the winter was in the hedgerow at the edge of Holiday Meadow. As she was a grass-spider she did not need to travel far before she came to a suitable place to stay.

Agalena's House

It took her from spring until fall to finish her house although it was all right to live in after the first few days. Even when it was done it was not much more than a floor and a back hall. The hall was a tube which led from her floor to the ground. It had two door-holes which were always open. When she felt timid she ran off her floor into her hall and then down to the ground as fast as her eight legs could carry her. She hid among the grass clumps until she felt like going up through her hall again. Her floor sloped a little toward the hole that opened into her tube-like hall. Altogether her home was somewhat funnel-shaped.

The stuff of which she built her home was silk. It all came out of her own body. It was made in her silk glands and forced through many fine spinning-tubes out where the spinning-organs (*spinnerets*) could use it. Her six spinnerets were at the tip of her body where they were placed near together somewhat like three pairs of little tails.

Of course while Agalena was a baby spider as she was when she left the egg-sac in the spring, she needed only a tiny floor and hall. So, at first, her "funnel" was very little indeed. By the time she had finished working on it, however, her floor measured about twelve inches across. It took a great many silk threads to spin so wide a web.

As the young spider grew, her plump body became crowded inside her firm skin. Then she ripped a hole in her tight old skin and crept out of it, finding herself in a new one which was more stretchy so that her body had room to grow. Later this new skin, in its turn, needed to be shed when it became too snug for comfort. She changed her skin several times before she was a fully grown spider.

Such a process of shedding skin is called molting. Spiders are not the only animals that molt this way as they grow. Other backbone-less animals with jointed legs, such as insects and crabs and crayfishes, also molt several times before they become full-grown.

After Agalena grew to be about three-fourths of an inch long she did not molt again. She was now yellow with dashes of pale gray here and there and with some long dark stripes and some light stripes on her body. She was a very good-looking spider.

This little eight-legged yellow and gray animal hunted for her living. She did not, however, take long hunting trips. She caught what she needed without leaving her own door-yard. Her favorite food was insect-juice. Because many of the insects she caught were injurious to grass, the man who owned Holiday Farm liked to have her hunting in his meadow.

She spent much of her time waiting in her narrow hall or runway. When an insect chanced to alight on her floor it jarred the silk a little. She could feel the very gentle shaking of her web and she would run out and capture a breakfast or luncheon or dinner for herself. She always hurried at such times as if she were excited.

She depended on the way her floor trembled when it was touched to know when her food arrived instead of watching with her eight eyes. And sometimes she was fooled.

Quite often Anne and Dick, the cousins from Holiday Farm, came to visit Agalena. One of them would touch her floor gently with a piece of stiff straw. Agalena would feel the quiver of the web and would rush out and grab the end of the straw. This game did the spider no real harm and it did give the children a chance to watch Agalena. They could see whether she had grown larger and how she looked after she had molted and had on a new suit of skin. They became much interested in the spider.

Agalena had spun strands of silk reaching from her floor to the twigs of a meadow-sweet bush that grew next her yard at the edge of the grass field. When insects blundered against these slender ropes of silk they often fell to the web beneath them where the spider could catch them easily.

The little hunter had a strange sort of appetite. When insects came to her web in great numbers she could eat the juices of all she caught and not feel overfed. But during days when she caught nothing at all, she did not starve. She could eat a great deal or very little indeed and could fast for long times. The size and time of her meals depended on how much food she caught and when she caught it.

When the men from the farm harvested the grass in the meadow, the hay-rake tore away part of Agalena's house. She soon mended her floor, however, and was as well off as before.

In the spring the young spider's small and dainty web hardly showed at all in the grass. Even in the summer, when the silk floor had been made thicker with many added threads of silk, a person could usually walk right past Agalena's yard without noticing her home. But on mornings after clear nights, during which heavy dew formed, her moist carpet glistened in the light.

It was easy, at such times, for Anne and Dick to learn something about the number of spiders in the

When dew is on the web it shows plainly.

meadow. For Agalena, of course, was not the only grass-spider living there. Thousands of webs like hers had been made during the spring and summer. After the hay was cut these could be seen, on a dewy morning, like little dainty white cloths spread in the field to dry.

In spite of all her neighbors, many of them, indeed, her sisters and cousins and other near relatives, Agalena lived alone until fall. But on a pleasant autumn day another grass-spider came to call on her. One of his names was Næ´-vi-a; and it was at this time that Miss Agalena became Mrs. Nævia.

Soon after this Mrs. Nævia left the silk home where she had grown and molted and hunted during so many weeks. She never returned to it. She was done with it forever. She had other matters to attend to now.

For the time had come when she must find a good place for her eggs. She wandered about until she reached a sheltered place beneath a piece of loose bark on a tree in the hedgerow. Here she laid her pretty round eggs and spun a fine firm sac about them. Over the sac she laid a sheet of silk, spinning it thread by thread as she moved back and forth. Next she scattered some tiny dark bits of bark over the white sheet. It did not show quite so plainly then.

Her important task was completed. Mother Agalena Nævia sat down beside the winter bed she had made for her egg babies and rested.

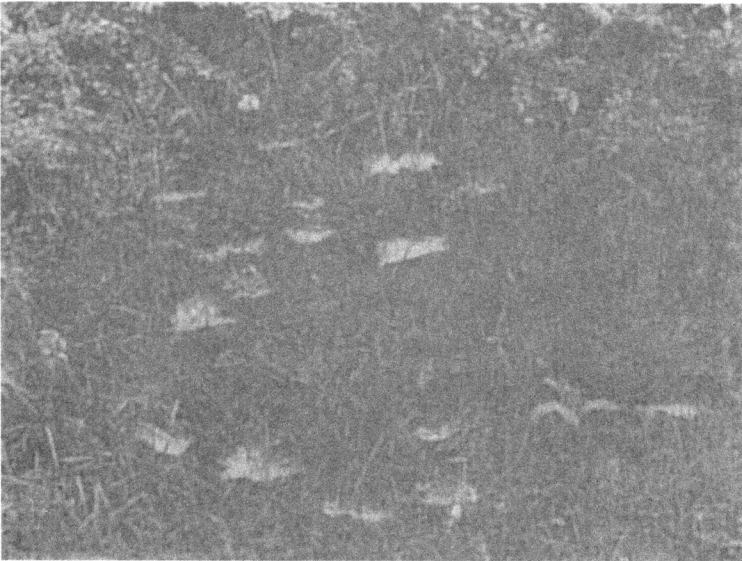

Spider webs in a grassy place.